HOW
HEINEMANN OUR WORLD

INVADERS *and Settlers*

JANE SHUTER
PAT TAYLOR

HEINEMANN EDUCATIONAL

Acknowledgements
The authors and publishers are grateful to the following for permission to reproduce copyright photographs:
pp. 9, 10, 14 — C.M. Dixon
pp. 15, 23—British Museum
p. 16—Archäologisches Landesmuseum Schleswig
p. 27—Werner Forman Archive
pp. 30-31—Michael Holford.

First published 1992
Designed by Miller, Craig & Cocking
Illustrated by Tony Maguire
Printed in Spain by Mateu Cromo Artes Graficas SA.

93 94 95 12 11 10 9 8 7 6 5 4

Heinemann Educational,
a division of Heinemann Educational Books Ltd,
Halley Court, Jordan Hill, Oxford OX2 8EJ.

OXFORD LONDON EDINBURGH
MADRID ATHENS BOLOGNA PARIS
MELBOURNE SYDNEY AUCKLAND SINGAPORE TOKYO
IBADAN NAIROBI HARARE GABORONE
PORTSMOUTH NH (USA)

0 435 04244 0 softback
0 435 04362 5 hardback

Contents

Introduction

The Romans, Anglo-Saxons and Vikings all invaded and settled in Britain. They brought new things and new ways of living. They were not the only peoples to invade and settle in Britain. There were Britons living here when the Romans invaded, and the Normans invaded after the Vikings. Each invasion affected only parts of Britain, not all of it. The chart on page 5 lists the most important things that happened at this time. It lists them in the order they happened.

The invasions did not come one after another. The Anglo-Saxons came when the Romans were still in power. The Vikings and the Anglo-Saxons were in Britain at the same time.

Britain was not the only place these peoples invaded. The different invaders had very similar reasons for invading and settling in other countries.

55 BC	Caesar first invaded Britain. He left when winter came.
54 BC	Caesar came again and defeated the British in the south-east. He left when winter came.
44 BC	Caesar was murdered.
AD 43	Claudius invaded Britain.
AD 61	Boudicca's revolt.
AD 122	Hadrian's Wall started. The south of Britain was mostly under Roman control.
AD 270	First raids by Anglo-Saxon pirates. The Romans were too strong for them.
AD 367	Romans raided by Anglo-Saxons, Picts and Scots at the same time.
AD 383	Some Anglo-Saxon settlement in Britain.
AD 410	Romans left Britain.
AD 450	British king, Vortigern, asked Anglo-Saxons Hengist and Horsa for help.
AD 476	Collapse of Western Roman Empire.
AD 550	Anglo-Saxons had seven kingdoms. Britons on the west coast and in Ireland.
AD 596	Christian conversion of Anglo-Saxons began.
AD 787	First Viking raids.
AD 841	Vikings settled in Ireland.
AD 866	First large Viking settlement in England.
AD 878	Alfred beat Guthrum. Danelaw created.
AD 948	Erik Bloodaxe, King of York.
AD 1013	Second Viking invasion (Swegn Forkbeard).
AD 1014–16	Ethelred the Unready.
AD 1017	A Viking, Canute, became king.
AD 1035	Canute died. His two sons ruled for just seven years.
AD 1042	Edward the Confessor became king.

The Romans invade Britain

The city of Rome was once very rich and strong. The Romans controlled a lot of countries. By AD 117 they ruled all the lands round the Mediterranean Sea, and many other parts of Europe. All of this was called the Roman Empire.

The Romans wanted to make their empire bigger and bigger. In 55 BC Julius Caesar led a Roman army to Britain. The people of Britain did not want the Romans in their land. They fought back. When winter came, the Romans had to leave. In 54 BC Julius Caesar and the Roman army came back. This time they took control of the south-east of Britain. Again, they left when winter came.

The Roman Empire in AD 117.

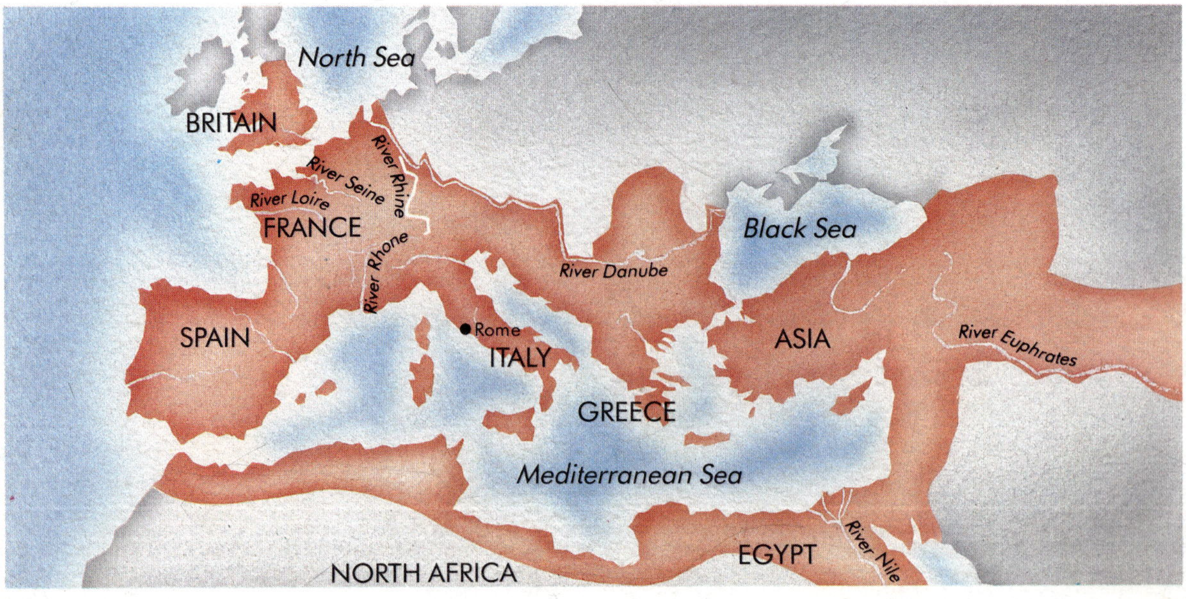

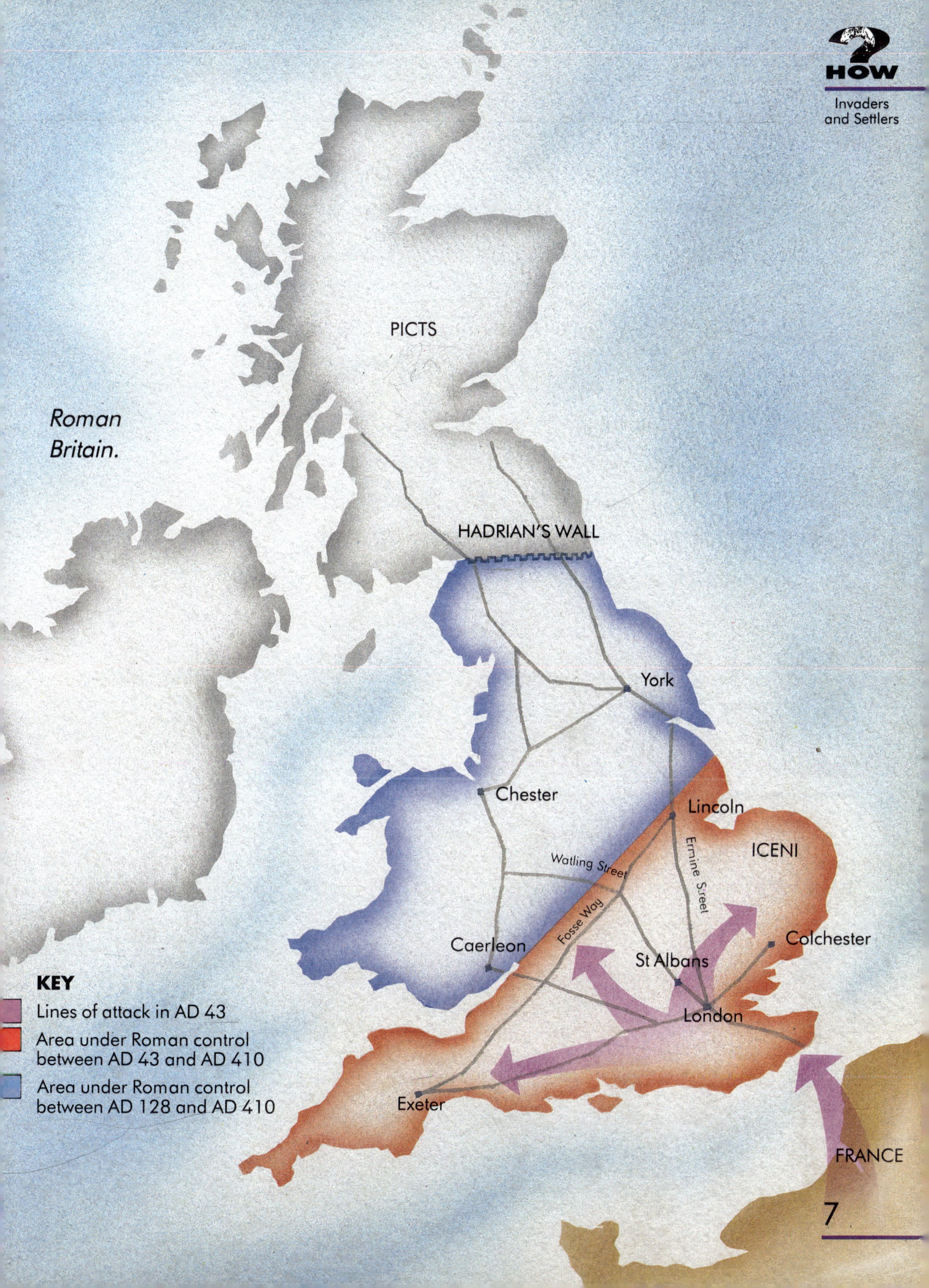

Roman Britain.

KEY

- Lines of attack in AD 43
- Area under Roman control between AD 43 and AD 410
- Area under Roman control between AD 128 and AD 410

The Romans settle in Britain

In AD 43, the army of the emperor Claudius landed in Kent. This army was much bigger. The soldiers were well trained. They had good weapons and armour. The Romans built good, straight roads to get the soldiers across the country quickly. They built camps and forts along the roads.

The Britons lived in many different tribes. They were not well organized and did not have many weapons, so they could not win against the Romans.

The Romans settled in Britain and built towns. They brought their way of life with them and changed many things.

This timeline shows when the Romans were in Britain.

BC

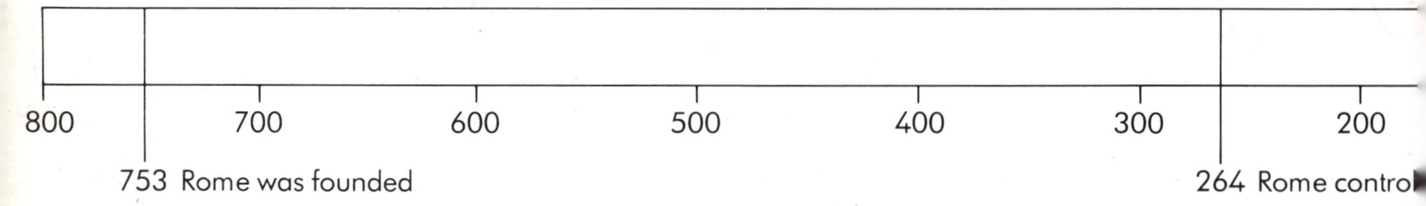

Roman soldiers and slaves building a road.

You can still see some Roman roads. This one is in Yorkshire.

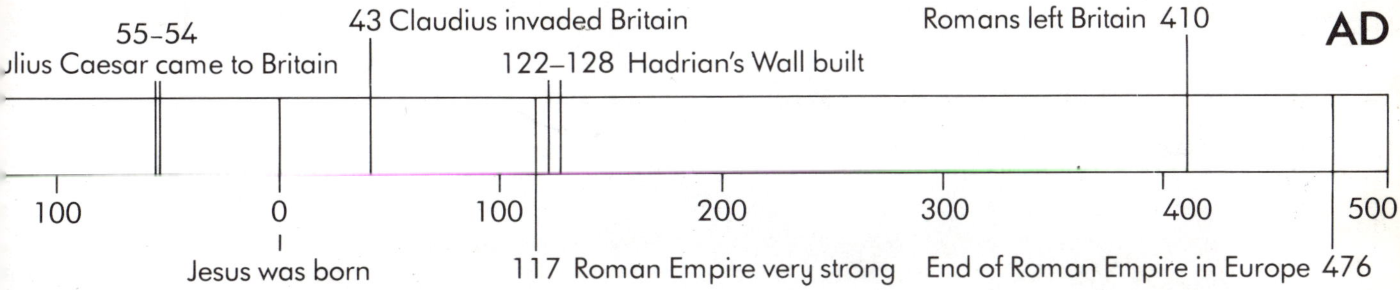

Resistance to the Romans

Caratacus and his tribe, the Catuvellauni, fought the Romans in AD 43. They lost, and Caratacus ran away. He was captured and taken to Rome.

In AD 61, the Iceni, a tribe living in the east of Britain, attacked some Roman towns and burned them. Their leader was a woman called Boudicca. All the people in the towns were killed. Other tribes joined the Iceni. The Romans then sent a big army. They beat the tribes. They rebuilt their towns.

In the area that we now call Scotland, the Romans had many battles with the Picts. In AD 122 Emperor Hadrian came to Britain. He made his army build a long wall to keep out the Picts.

This is Hadrian's Wall. There were many forts along it and hundreds of soldiers guarded it. Board games and dice have been found here.

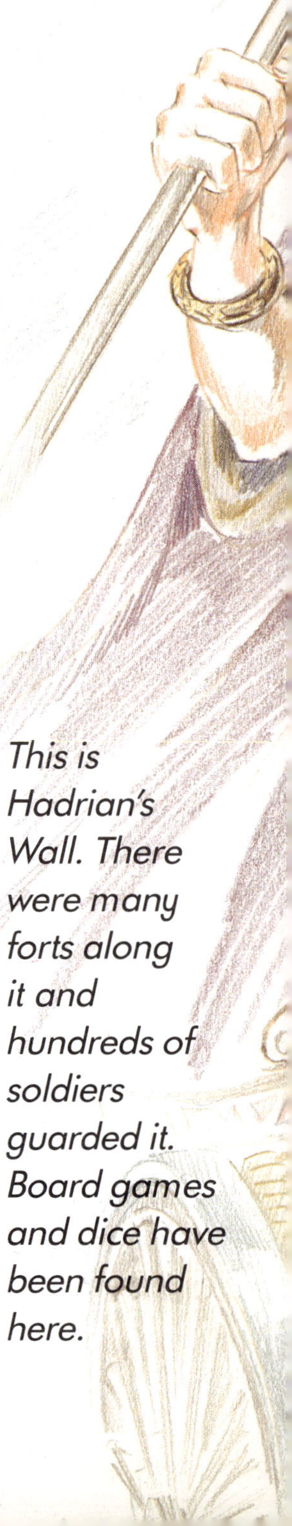

This is a description of Boudicca by Cassius Dio, a Greek historian who lived in Rome.

She was very tall, in appearance she was most terrifying. Her eye was fierce and her voice was harsh. A great mass of red hair fell to her hips. Around her neck was a large golden necklace. She wore a tunic of many colours. Over this was a thick cloak, fastened with a brooch. She held a spear to help her look more terrifying.

This is how Boudicca may have looked as she fought the Roman soldiers.

Everyday life in Roman Britain

Many Romans lived in towns. There were many buildings which everyone could use. Most houses were quite small, and some were split into flats called insulae. Richer people lived in larger houses. Out of the towns, most people lived on farms. Rich people lived in big houses called villas, or on estates which had a lot of land.

Everyone ate bread, fruit and vegetables. They drank wine. Richer people ate fish, meat and sometimes small birds.

The men worked and the women looked after the house. They both had slaves to help them. Boys, and some girls, learned to read and write.

Many Britons copied the Roman way of life. They began to think of themselves as Romans. Britons who followed the Roman ways were given jobs, and had a much easier life than those who tried to live as Britons.

A Roman town.

The Romans leave Britain

The Roman Empire was very big. It was hard to defend all of it. By AD 300 many tribes were attacking it. Roman soldiers were needed in other parts of the Empire. They started to leave Britain. By AD 410, all of the Roman soldiers had gone.

The Romans were in Britain for about 400 years. They changed many things. They decorated their houses with mosaics and paintings. They built fine roads and buildings. They were traders and helped people to buy and sell many things. Many people became Christians after Emperor Constantine was converted.

A painting of a Roman ship. The ship was called the Isis Giminiana.

As the Empire grew weak, and the soldiers left, things were not run so well. Anglo-Saxons, who had been trading with the Romans, saw that the Romans were getting weaker. They began to raid, and take what they wanted, instead of trading.

This mosaic was part of the floor of a villa. It shows the head of Jesus.

Who were the Anglo-Saxons?

The Anglo-Saxons were many different tribes. These included the Angles, the Saxons and the Jutes. They came from parts of Europe that were close to each other. They had similar languages and ways of life. This meant that many people thought they were the same.

The Anglo-Saxons first came to Britain as soldiers in the Roman army, or as traders. Later, some raided the coast. The first Anglo-Saxon settlers were given land by the Romans in return for helping to defend Britain against other raiders. When the Romans left, more Anglo-Saxons came. They settled, mostly on land that no one was using, in the south and east.

An Anglo-Saxon ship. It was found in Nydam in Germany.

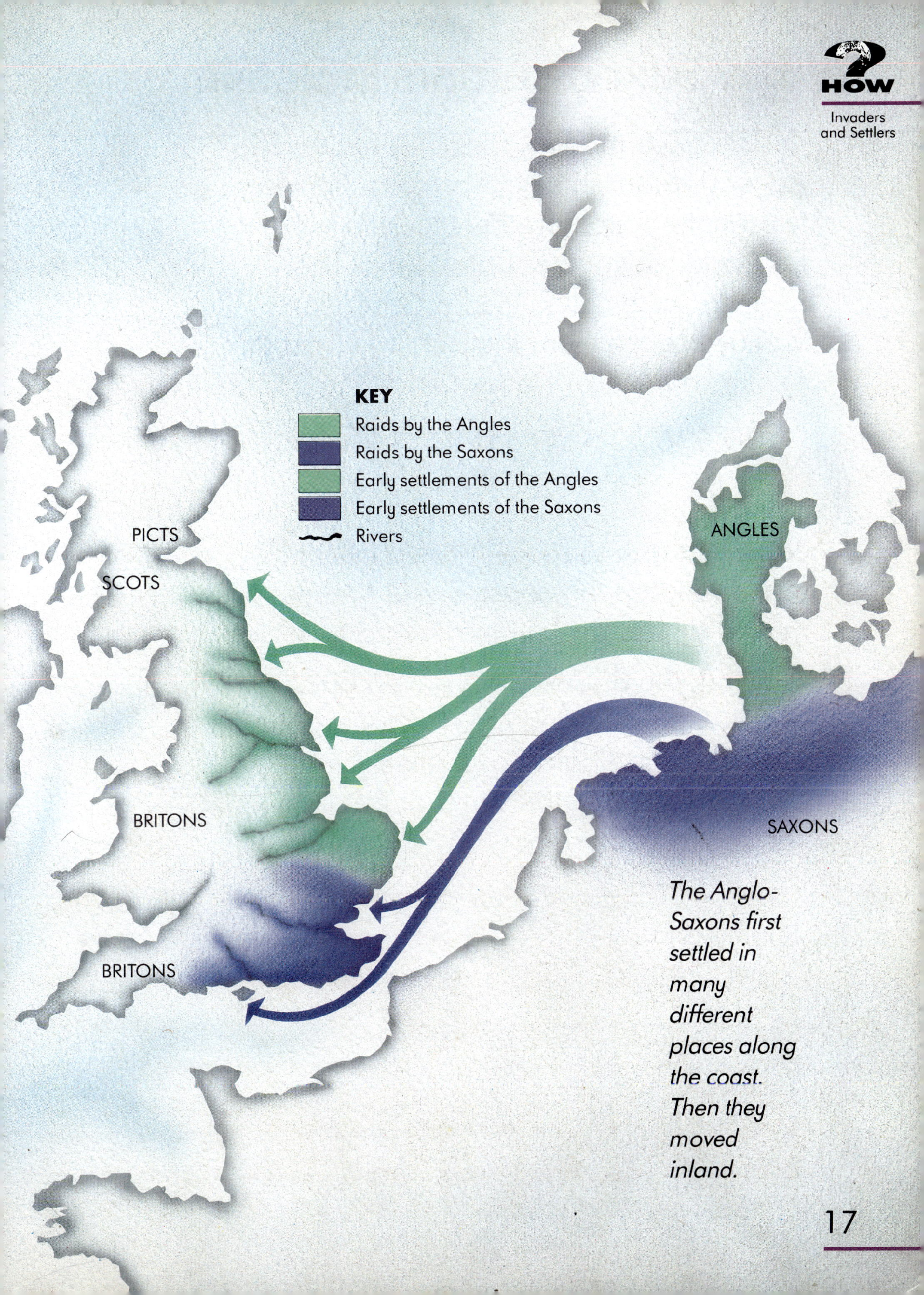

The Anglo-Saxons first settled in many different places along the coast. Then they moved inland.

Anglo-Saxon settlers in Britain

There are many stories that say that in AD 450, a British king, Vortigern, asked two Anglo-Saxon brothers to help him fight against another British king. The brothers were called Hengist and Horsa. Vortigern gave them the Isle of Thanet in Kent as a reward. Hengist and Horsa soon took over and Hengist was made king of Kent.

From then on, more and more Anglo-Saxons began to settle in Britain. At first, they settled on the coast. Some of them moved further and further inland to settle.

Soon, the Britons were driven back to Wales, Cornwall and the north-west of England. The Anglo-Saxons were in control of most of the south of Britain. They called it England.

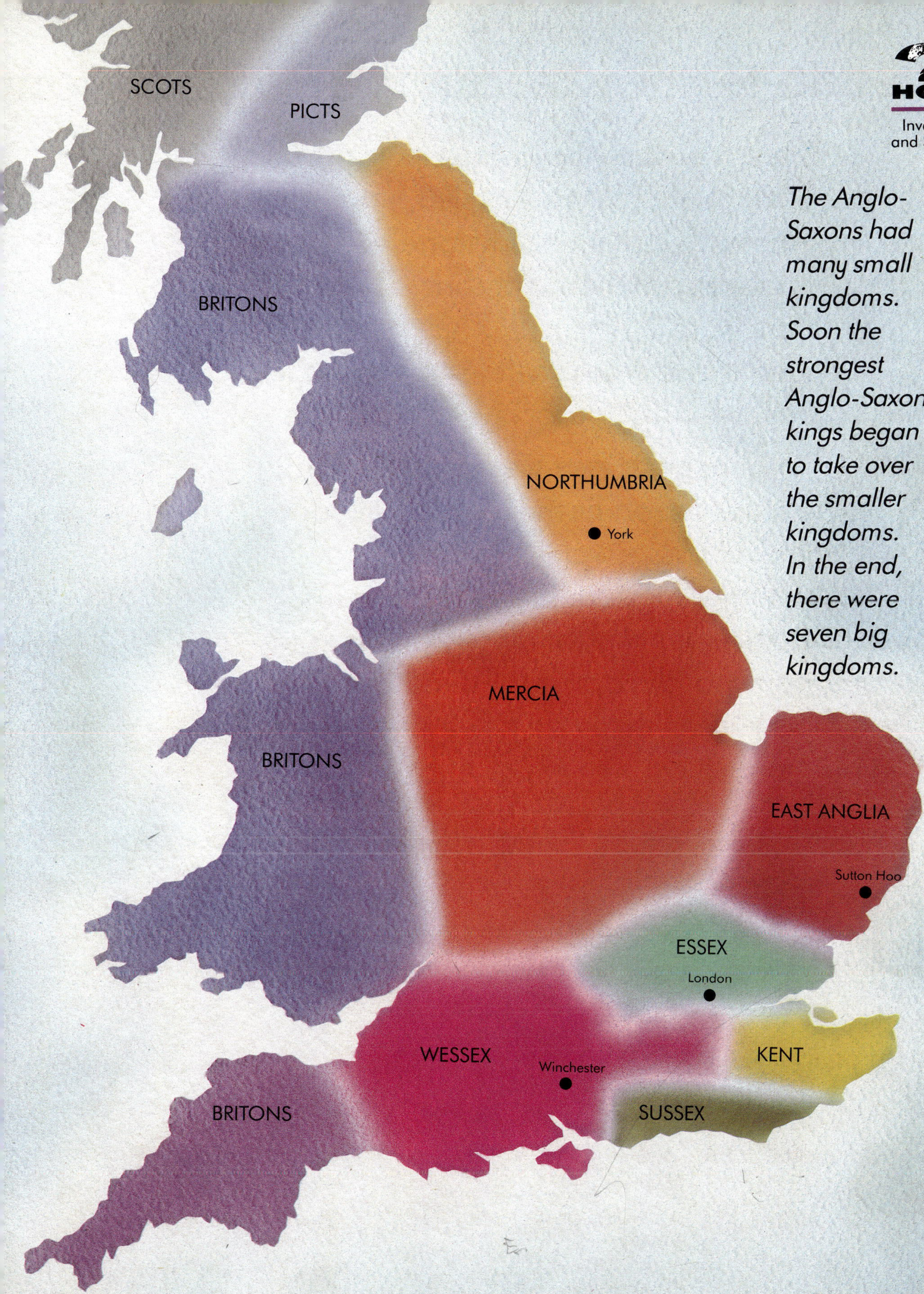

The Anglo-Saxons had many small kingdoms. Soon the strongest Anglo-Saxon kings began to take over the smaller kingdoms. In the end, there were seven big kingdoms.

How we know about the Anglo-Saxons

To see how the Anglo-Saxons lived we must look at the things they left behind. They did not want to build stone houses or make mosaics like the Romans. They built thatched wooden houses. They made beautiful things from metal. Archaeologists have found many brooches and buckles.

Archaeologists can find out a lot about how Anglo-Saxon homes were built, and how their villages were organized, by excavating village sites. The problem is that wooden things rot away. It is hard to find out what the houses looked like. As archaeologists excavate more sites, they find more clues.

Anglo-Saxon family groups ate and slept in their hall.

How Anglo-Saxon life changed

When they first came to Britain, few Anglo-Saxons wanted to read or write. Their enemies, British monks, wrote about them at the time. The Anglo-Saxons told stories over and over. We still know these stories. They might tell us something about Anglo-Saxon life, but the stories may have changed as they were passed on.

The Anglo-Saxons did not live in the same way all the time. The most important change in the lives of many of them was that they became Christians. They also built a navy, set up schools to teach more people to read and write, and built walled towns called burghs.

The barbarians drive us to the sea and the sea drives us back to the barbarians. One way or another we die, we are either killed or drowned.

This was written by a monk called Gildas in about AD 466. He was complaining to Rome about Anglo-Saxon invasions.

Many of these changes came under King Alfred, one of the most important Anglo-Saxon kings. It was Alfred who finally made peace with the Vikings. He also converted Guthrum, the leader of the biggest Viking group, to Christianity.

A picture from an Anglo-Saxon book. It shows their idea of a Viking ship.

The Vikings

The Vikings came from Norway and Denmark. At first, they raided Britain. They came, took want they wanted, and went home. Later, their families came to settle.

The Norwegian and Danish Vikings probably thought of themselves as different people. They raided and settled in different places. Peace treaties with one group of Vikings did not stop another group from raiding. Some people saw all Vikings as fierce raiders from the North. We have been told most about them by those who were their enemies.

Once the Vikings decided to settle, they fitted into new countries very quickly. The lives of Vikings in Britain were very similar to those of the Anglo-Saxons.

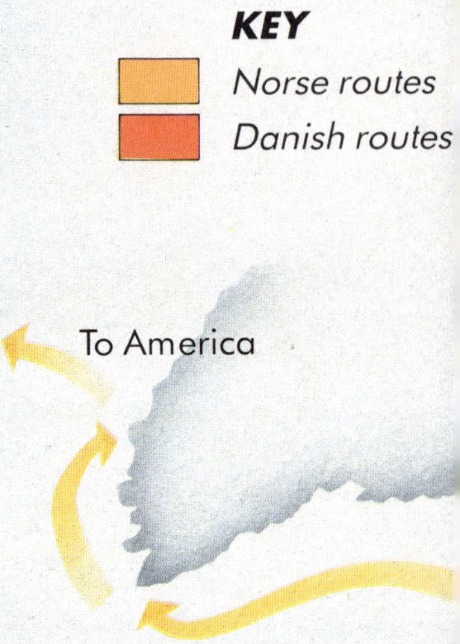

The army raided here and there and filled every place with bloodshed and sorrow. Far and wide they destroyed churches and monasteries with fire and sword. They left nothing standing but roofless walls.

This was written by an English monk, Simon of Durham, in AD 856.

The Vikings raided Britain between AD 787 and AD 800. After this they began to settle.

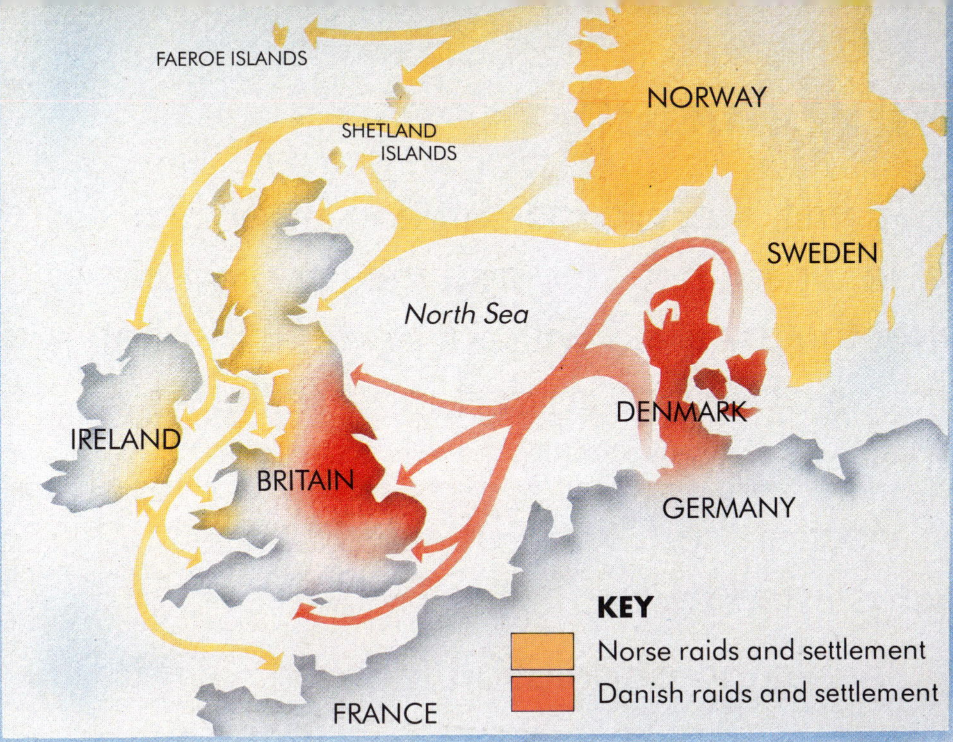

The Vikings settled in many countries.

Viking raiders

At first, the Vikings came to Britain to trade. Then they saw that they could take what they wanted without trade. Different groups of Vikings raided, and settled, for different reasons.

Most of them were affected by the things listed below:

- The Viking population (number of people) was growing fast. More and more people were trying to live off the same amount of land.

A Viking longship. These were bigger and faster than the ships used for trading or for bringing settlers. They were used for raiding.

- Their land was difficult to farm. It was hard to grow enough food. If there was a bad winter, they often had to eat seaweed, bark and lichen, and whatever they could catch in the sea.
- The Vikings saw raiding as part of their way of life.
- The Vikings wanted to find new places to trade with.
- The Vikings wanted new bases so that they could invade more lands.

Much of the land in Norway and Denmark is steep and rocky, or wet and marshy, and the weather is very harsh.

Viking settlers

Some reasons why the Vikings settled in Britain are shown on page 26. They mostly settled in places where they did not have to fight for the land. They also chose places from where they could reach their homeland easily. Some Vikings settled in Ireland, around Dublin. Another big town was Jorvik, now called York. Here, a strong Viking settlement grew up.

The Vikings came with their own ways of doing things, and their own religion. Later, they mixed in with the local people and took on some of their ways. Many of them changed their religion and became Christians.

Early Viking homes, in towns and in small villages, looked like this.

Invaders of Britain

Romans, Anglo-Saxons and Vikings all invaded and settled in Britain. They brought new things and new ways of living. They also changed, to fit in with the local ways. The Romans settled the most land, and changed their ways the least. The Anglo-Saxons and the Vikings, who were in Britain at the same time, shared some gods and many customs. They changed more, to fit in.

The Normans landing in Britain. This is part of the Bayeux Tapestry, which was made at that time.

There was no sudden end to the Viking invasions. They attacked whenever the country looked weak. Sometimes a Viking, or someone who was part Viking (like King Canute) would take over from the Anglo-Saxons.

The Anglo-Saxon and Viking power struggle was ended by another invasion. In AD 1066 the Normans invaded. Look at the picture here and the map on page 25. Who were the Normans descended from?

Index